Autonomous Maintenance Form

Location: _____

Equipment: _____

Group: _____
Leader: _____
Tag No: _____

Prepared: _____
Revised: _____

T0111895

Inspecting Sequence

Part	Standard	Method	Tool	Action if abnormal	Time (min)	Dy	Wk	Mo	Yr	Resp.
Inspection Time required (min)										

LUBRICATION

Lube point	Lube type	Method	Lube qty	Tool	Time (min)	Dy	Wk	Mo	Yr	Resp.
Lubrication Time required (min)										

© ENNA
KNOWLEDGE INTO PRACTICE
www.enna.com
www.productivitypress.com

LEGEND: Visually inspect 👁 Listen 👂 Touch 👆 Smell 👃

Autonomous Maintenance Form

Location: _____

Equipment: _____

Group: _____
Leader: _____
Tag No: _____

Prepared: _____
Revised: _____

Inspecting Sequence

Part	Standard	Method	Tool	Action if abnormal	Time (min)	Dy	Wk	Mo	Yr	Resp.
				Inspection Time required (min)						

Interval: Dy | Wk | Mo | Yr

LUBRICATION

Lube point	Lube type	Method	Lube qty	Tool	Time (min)	Dy	Wk	Mo	Yr	Resp.
					Lubrication Time required (min)					

Interval: Dy | Wk | Mo | Yr

LEGEND: **Visually inspect** 👁   Listen 👂   Touch ✋   Smell 👃

Autonomous Maintenance Form

Location:		Equipment:	Group:	Prepared:
			Leader:	Revised:
			Tag No:	

Inspecting Sequence

Part	Standard	Method	Tool	Action if abnormal	Time (min)	Interval Dy	Wk	Mo	Yr	Resp.
Inspection Time required (min)										

LUBRICATION

Lube point	Lube type	Method	Lube qty	Tool	Time (min)	Interval Dy	Wk	Mo	Yr	Resp.
Lubrication Time required (min)										

LEGEND: Visually inspect 👁   Listen 👂   Touch ✋   Smell 👃

Autonomous Maintenance Form

Location: _____ Equipment: _____

Group: _____ Prepared: _____
Leader: _____
Tag No: _____ Revised: _____

Inspecting Sequence

Part	Standard	Method	Tool	Action if abnormal	Time (min)	Dy	Wk	Mo	Yr	Resp.
				Inspection Time required (min)						

LUBRICATION

Lube point	Lube type	Method	Lube qty	Tool	Time (min)	Dy	Wk	Mo	Yr	Resp.
					Lubrication Time required (min)					

KNOWLEDGE INTO PRACTICE

www.enna.com
www.productivitypress.com

LEGEND: Visually inspect   Listen   Touch   Smell

Autonomous Maintenance Form

Location: _____		Equipment: _____	Group: _____ Leader: _____ Tag No: _____	Prepared: _____ Revised: _____

Inspecting Sequence

	Part	Standard	Method	Tool	Action if abnormal	Time (min)	Interval				Resp.
							Dy	Wk	Mo	Yr	
						Inspection Time required (min)					

LUBRICATION

	Lube point	Lube type	Method	Lube qty	Tool	Time (min)	Interval				Resp.
							Dy	Wk	Mo	Yr	
						Lubrication Time required (min)					

LEGEND: Visually inspect 👁 Listen 👂 Touch ✋ Smell 👃

Autonomous Maintenance Form

Location: _____

Equipment: _____

Group: _____
Leader: _____
Tag No: _____

Prepared: _____
Revised: _____

Inspecting Sequence

Part	Standard	Method	Tool	Action if abnormal	Time (min)	Interval				Resp.
						Dy	Wk	Mo	Yr	
Inspection Time required (min)										

LUBRICATION

Lube point	Lube type	Method	Lube qty	Tool	Time (min)	Interval				Resp.
						Dy	Wk	Mo	Yr	
Lubrication Time required (min)										

LEGEND: **Visually inspect** 👁   **Listen** 👂   **Touch** 👆   **Smell** 👃

Autonomous Maintenance Form

Group:_____   Prepared:_____

Leader:_____   Revised:_____

Tag No:_____

Location: _____   Equipment:_____

Inspecting Sequence

Part	Standard	Method	Tool	Action if abnormal	Time (min)	Dy	Wk	Mo	Yr	Resp.
Inspection Time required (min)										

LUBRICATION

Lube point	Lube type	Method	Lube qty	Tool	Time (min)	Dy	Wk	Mo	Yr	Resp.
Lubrication Time required (min)										

LEGEND: Visually inspect 👁   Listen 👂   Touch   Smell 👃

Autonomous Maintenance Form

Location: _____ **Equipment:** _____

Group: _____ **Leader:** _____ **Tag No:** _____

Prepared: _____ **Revised:** _____

Inspecting Sequence

Part	Standard	Method	Tool	Action if abnormal	Time (min)	Interval Dy	Wk	Mo	Yr	Resp.
Inspection Time required (min)										

LUBRICATION

Lube point	Lube type	Method	Lube qty	Tool	Time (min)	Interval Dy	Wk	Mo	Yr	Resp.
Lubrication Time required (min)										

© ENNA KNOWLEDGE INTO PRACTICE

www.enna.com
www.productivitypress.com

LEGEND: Visually inspect 👁 Listen 👂 Touch ✋ Smell 👃

Autonomous Maintenance Form

Location: _____   Equipment: _____

Group: _____   Prepared: _____
Leader: _____   Revised: _____
Tag No: _____

Inspecting Sequence

Part	Standard	Method	Tool	Action if abnormal	Time (min)	Dy	Wk	Mo	Yr	Resp.
				Inspection Time required (min)						

LUBRICATION

Lube point	Lube type	Method	Lube qty	Tool	Time (min)	Dy	Wk	Mo	Yr	Resp.
					Lubrication Time required (min)					

LEGEND: Visually inspect 👁   Listen 👂   Touch ☝   Smell 👃

Autonomous Maintenance Form

Location: _____	Equipment: _____	Group: _____	Prepared: _____
		Leader: _____	Revised: _____
		Tag No: _____	

Inspecting Sequence

	Part	Standard	Method	Tool	Action if abnormal	Time (min)	Dy	Wk	Mo	Yr	Resp.
				Inspection Time required (min)							

LUBRICATION

	Lube point	Lube type	Method	Lube qty	Tool	Time (min)	Dy	Wk	Mo	Yr	Resp.
					Lubrication Time required (min)						

LEGEND: Visually inspect 👁 Listen 👂 Touch 👆 Smell 👃

Autonomous Maintenance Form

Group: _____	Prepared: _____
Leader: _____	
Tag No: _____	Revised: _____

Location: _____

Equipment: _____

Inspecting Sequence

Part	Standard	Method	Tool	Action if abnormal	Time (min)	Interval Dy	Wk	Mo	Yr	Resp.
Inspection Time required (min)										

LUBRICATION

Lube point	Lube type	Method	Lube qty	Tool	Time (min)	Interval Dy	Wk	Mo	Yr	Resp.
Lubrication Time required (min)										

LEGEND: **Visually inspect** 👁   Listen 👂   Touch ✋   Smell 👃

Autonomous Maintenance Form

Location: _____

Equipment: _____

Group: _____

Leader: _____

Tag No: _____

Prepared: _____

Revised: _____

Inspecting Sequence

Part	Standard	Method	Tool	Action if abnormal	Time (min)	Dy	Wk	Mo	Yr	Resp.
Inspection Time required (min)										

LUBRICATION

Lube point	Lube type	Method	Lube qty	Tool	Time (min)	Dy	Wk	Mo	Yr	Resp.
Lubrication Time required (min)										

LEGEND: Visually inspect 👁 Listen 👂 Touch 👆 Smell 👃

Autonomous Maintenance Form

Location: _____ Equipment: _____

Group: _____ Prepared: _____
Leader: _____
Tag No: _____ Revised: _____

Inspecting Sequence

Part	Standard	Method	Tool	Action if abnormal	Time (min)	Dy	Wk	Mo	Yr	Resp.
				Inspection Time required (min)						

LUBRICATION

Lube point	Lube type	Method	Lube qty	Tool	Time (min)	Dy	Wk	Mo	Yr	Resp.
					Lubrication Time required (min)					

LEGEND: Visually inspect 👁 Listen 👂 Touch 👆 Smell 👃

Autonomous Maintenance Form

Location: _____

Equipment: _____

Group: _____

Leader: _____

Tag No: _____

Prepared: _____

Revised: _____

Inspecting Sequence

Part	Standard	Method	Tool	Action if abnormal	Time (min)	Dy	Wk	Mo	Yr	Resp.
				Inspection Time required (min)						

LUBRICATION

Lube point	Lube type	Method	Lube qty	Tool	Time (min)	Dy	Wk	Mo	Yr	Resp.
				Lubrication Time required (min)						

© ENNA
KNOWLEDGE INTO PRACTICE
www.enna.com
www.productivitypress.com

LEGEND: Visually inspect 👁 Listen 👂 Touch Smell 👃

Autonomous Maintenance Form

Location: _____	Equipment: _____	Group: _____ Leader: _____ Tag No: _____	Prepared: _____ Revised: _____

Inspecting Sequence

	Part	Standard	Method	Tool	Action if abnormal	Time (min)	Interval Dy	Wk	Mo	Yr	Resp.
						Inspection Time required (min)					

LUBRICATION

	Lube point	Lube type	Method	Lube qty	Tool	Time (min)	Interval Dy	Wk	Mo	Yr	Resp.
						Lubrication Time required (min)					

LEGEND: Visually inspect 👁 Listen 👂 Touch ✋ Smell 👃

Autonomous Maintenance Form

Group:_____ Prepared:_____
Leader:_____ Revised:_____
Tag No:_____

Location:_____ Equipment:_____

Inspecting Sequence

Part	Standard	Method	Tool	Action if abnormal	Time (min)	Dy	Wk	Mo	Yr	Resp.
				Inspection Time required (min)						

LUBRICATION

Lube point	Lube type	Method	Lube qty	Tool	Time (min)	Dy	Wk	Mo	Yr	Resp.
				Lubrication Time required (min)						

© ENNA
KNOWLEDGE INTO PRACTICE
www.enna.com
www.productivitypress.com

LEGEND: Visually inspect 👁 Listen 👂 Touch ✋ Smell 👃

Autonomous Maintenance Form

Location: _____ Equipment: _____

Group: _____ Prepared: _____
Leader: _____
Tag No: _____ Revised: _____

Inspecting Sequence

Part	Standard	Method	Tool	Action if abnormal	Time (min)	Dy	Wk	Mo	Yr	Resp.
				Inspection Time required (min)						

LUBRICATION

Lube point	Lube type	Method	Lube qty	Tool	Time (min)	Dy	Wk	Mo	Yr	Resp.

LEGEND: Visually inspect 👁 Listen 👂 Touch 👆 Smell 👃

Lubrication Time required (min)

Autonomous Maintenance Form

Location:		Equipment:		Group:	Prepared:
				Leader:	
				Tag No:	Revised:

Inspecting Sequence

Part	Standard	Method	Tool	Action if abnormal	Time (min)	Interval				Resp.
						Dy	Wk	Mo	Yr	
Inspection Time required (min)										

LUBRICATION

Lube point	Lube type	Method	Lube qty	Tool	Time (min)	Interval				Resp.
						Dy	Wk	Mo	Yr	
Lubrication Time required (min)										

LEGEND: Visually inspect 👁 Listen 👂 Touch ✋ Smell 👃

Autonomous M intenanc Form

Location: _____

Equipment: _____

Group: _____ **Prepared:** _____

Leader: _____ **Revised:** _____

Tag No: _____

Inspecting Sequence

Part	Standard	Method	Tool	Action if abnormal	Time (min)	Dy	Wk	Mo	Yr	Resp.
				Inspection Time required (min)						

LUBRICATION

Lube point	Lube type	Method	Lube qty	Tool	Time (min)	Dy	Wk	Mo	Yr	Resp.
					Lubrication Time required (min)					

LEGEND: Visually inspect 👁 Listen 👂 Touch 👆 Smell 👃

Autonomous Maintenance Form

| Location: _____ | | Equipment: _____ | | Group: _____
 Leader: _____
 Tag No: _____ | | Prepared: _____

 Revised: _____ |

Inspecting Sequence

	Part	Standard	Method	Tool	Action if abnormal	Time (min)	Interval				Resp.
							Dy	Wk	Mo	Yr	
			Inspection Time required (min)								

LUBRICATION

	Lube point	Lube type	Method	Lube qty	Tool	Time (min)	Interval				Resp.
							Dy	Wk	Mo	Yr	
				Lubrication Time required (min)							

LEGEND: Visually inspect 👁   Listen 👂   Touch   Smell 👃

Autonomous Maintenance Form

Group: _____   Prepared: _____
Leader: _____
Location: _____   Equipment: _____   Tag No: _____   Revised: _____

Inspecting Sequence

Part	Standard	Method	Tool	Action if abnormal	Time (min)	Dy	Wk	Mo	Yr	Resp.
				Inspection Time required (min)						

Interval columns: Dy, Wk, Mo, Yr

LUBRICATION

Lube point	Lube type	Method	Lube qty	Tool	Time (min)	Dy	Wk	Mo	Yr	Resp.
				Lubrication Time required (min)						

Interval columns: Dy, Wk, Mo, Yr

© ENNA
KNOWLEDGE INTO PRACTICE
www.enna.com
www.productivitypress.com

LEGEND: Visually inspect 👁   Listen 👂   Touch 👆   Smell 👃

Autonomous Maintenance Form

Group:_____ **Prepared:**_____

Leader:_____

Location: _____ **Equipment:** _____ **Tag No:**_____ **Revised:**_____

Inspecting Sequence

Part	Standard	Method	Tool	Action if abnormal	Time (min)	Interval				Resp.
						Dy	Wk	Mo	Yr	
Inspection Time required (min)										

LUBRICATION

Lube point	Lube type	Method	Lube qty	Tool	Time (min)	Interval				Resp.
						Dy	Wk	Mo	Yr	
Lubrication Time required (min)										

© ENNA
KNOWLEDGE INTO PRACTICE
www.enna.com
www.productivitypress.com

LEGEND: Visually inspect 👁 Listen 👂 Touch 👆 Smell 👃

Autonomous Maintenance Form

Location: _____		Equipment: _____		Group: _____		Prepared: _____
			Leader: _____		Revised: _____
			Tag No: _____		

Inspecting Sequence

Part	Standard	Method	Tool	Action if abnormal	Time (min)	Interval Dy	Wk	Mo	Yr	Resp.
Inspection Time required (min)										

LUBRICATION

Lube point	Lube type	Method	Lube qty	Tool	Time (min)	Interval Dy	Wk	Mo	Yr	Resp.
Lubrication Time required (min)										

LEGEND: Visually inspect 👁   Listen 👂   Touch 👆   Smell 👃

Autonomous Maintenance Form

Location: _____

Group: _____ Prepared: _____
Leader: _____
Tag No: _____ Revised: _____

Equipment: _____

Inspecting Sequence

Part	Standard	Method	Tool	Action if abnormal	Time (min)	Dy	Wk	Mo	Yr	Resp.
Inspection Time required (min)										

LUBRICATION

Lube point	Lube type	Method	Lube qty	Tool	Time (min)	Dy	Wk	Mo	Yr	Resp.
Lubrication Time required (min)										

LEGEND: Visually inspect 👁 Listen 👂 Touch 👆 Smell 👃

Autonomous Maintenance Form

Location: _____

Equipment: _____

Group: _____
Leader: _____
Tag No: _____

Prepared: _____
Revised: _____

Inspecting Sequence

Part	Standard	Method	Tool	Action if abnormal	Time (min)	Dy	Wk	Mo	Yr	Resp.
				Inspection Time required (min)						

(Interval columns: Dy, Wk, Mo, Yr)

LUBRICATION

Lube point	Lube type	Method	Lube qty	Tool	Time (min)	Dy	Wk	Mo	Yr	Resp.
				Lubrication Time required (min)						

(Interval columns: Dy, Wk, Mo, Yr)

LEGEND: Visually inspect 👁   Listen 👂   Touch 👆   Smell 👃